# THE CLARITY F1RST

An "unputdownable" book to gain true clarity, build more confidence & accelerate business growth

# THE CLARITY F1RST

An "unputdownable" book to gain true clarity, build more confidence & accelerate business growth

**AMIT CHAWLA**

*INDIA'S #1 BUSINESS CLARITY COACH*

Worldwide Published by

**Pendown** Press

**PENDOWN PRESS**
**An ISO 9001 & ISO 14001 Certified Co.,**
**Regd. Office:** 2525/193, 1st Floor, Onkar Nagar-A,
Tri Nagar, Delhi-110035
**Ph.:** 09350849407, 09312235086
**E-mail:** info@pendownpress.com
**Branch Office:** 1A/2A, 20, Hari Sadan, Ansari Road,
Daryaganj, New Delhi-110002
**Ph.:** 011-45794768
**Website**: PendownPress.com

**First Edition:** 2020
**Price:** ₹279/-
**ISBN:** 978-81-941269-3-5



*Layout and Cover Designed by* Pendown Graphics Team
*Printed and Bound in India by* Thomson Press India Ltd.

*"Nobody is better positioned to write a book about having clarity in business and in life than a notable clarity expert Amit Chawla. It is a unique book of tremendous value. I included it in the mandatory reading list for both senior and middle management."*

*–(Ritesh Malik, co-founder - Innov8)*

# Contents

# Dedicated to...

*My children, Abhinav and Drishti, who have kept me young in mind, body and heart.*

*And my wife, Deepika, for giving me reasons to smile each day...*

# Praises for this Book

*"The Clarity First" is a must read for anyone interested in changing their life - and fast. It is an eye-opening book that, if you let it, will change your life, forever. Thank you Amit Sir for penning such a wonderful book.*

*–(Shobhit Banga, co-founder –Josh Talks)*

*"The Clarity First" book is much more than your typical "self-help" personal development books! It is much more than that. In this book Amit has shared real insight and real tools to help you get clarity and move away from the web of uncertainty and obscurity that stop you from living your best life.*

*–(Rajesh Garodia, Pro-Vice Chancellor, Ashoka University)*

*This is an important, thought-provoking book. This is actually the first book that I've read that has acknowledged the importance of clarity in very existence of the business. This should be a required reading for all executives and business leaders.*

*–(Sarika Gupta Bhattacharyya,*
*Founder and CEO - BeyonDiversity)*

*Amit Chawla has clearly identified a fundamental block that limits many from achieving success. This book is a commendable step towards helping people identify and over their blind spots that often come in the way of achieving one's true potential.*

*- (Paritosh Pathak, Strategic*
*Networking Coach)*

# Preface

> ***"The purpose of life is a Life of purpose!"***
> ***— Robert Byrne***

It was $10^{th}$ September 2016, relaxed weekend day-Saturday. My family members, friends and relatives were celebrating my $50^{th}$ birthday (that was on $8^{th}$ Sep.) at our home in Faridabad. We had called close friends and colleagues. Big cake was there to be cut that had a lonely candle saved from my $1^{st}$ birthday by my mom. Champagne bottles were popped.

I cut the cake. Thunderous claps filled the air. Drinks, dance and dinner followed. Celebrations began. And I was 50. But I was not aware what was changing! I was in Software Industry at a Senior Leadership Position in an MNC and had a stable, well-paid job. Wife was working at a good position in another MNC son was in engineering college and daughter in $12^{th}$ standard".

But there was something missing and I was not sure what the hell that was! It took 10 years' struggle to find out that "missing"! Now, when I look back, I am clear that I was missing "Clarity". Since then, I have gone through a major transformation in my life and still continuing.

### It has made me

And it was really meant for me and inspiring me every day, to move in the direction that I love.

During this transformational journey, I have come across so many people who think they have something great to offer but they have no clarity about it. As I analyse it now, I find there are people who have lots of:

- Money, but no clarity of where and how to use it!
- Skill, but no clarity of where it can be utilised best!
- Experience, but no clarity of where can it be applied for achievement!
- Motivation and energy, but no clarity about how to best use these forces!
- Knowledge and immense information, but no clarity of what best to use it for!
- Power, to influence many lives, but no clarity about how to exercise this power in a great manner!
- Creativity, but no clarity of what to really create and how to put it for optimum results!
- Potential, but no clarity of how and where to put it to attain fulfilment in Life!

> ***"It's a lack of clarity that creates chaos and frustration. Those emotions are poison to any living goal."***
>
> ***— Steve Maraboli***

This ill-founded notion gives me immense pain as such people have all that is required to bring a major change in the world, yet they are not even aware that they need Clarity First (to do that ). In fact, they need clarity of what they really want to achieve in their lives, First, by all possible means.

So, my mission is to help them get Clarity First so that they can move on to achieve bigger goals and bring transformation in the World.

Well, I am writing this book as part of this mission so that more and more people get benefitted by it and make this World a better place to live in.

Wish you a Happy Reading...

# Acknowledgements

First and foremost, I would like to thank my parents, who gave me abundant love and nurturing environment during my childhood years. That enabled me to be self-confident and independent

I want to thank **Shobhit Banga and Cathy Nicholls** for triggering a thought in me of writing a book 2 years back.

I would like to thank **Col Sunil Prem** for giving me that initial confidence to start the process of writing the book when I was stuck in taking even the first step.

I would like to thank **Akshar Yadav** for being a great mentor and pushing me hard to complete the book. Also thanks to his brilliant team members **—Pankaj Bengani and Palak Mehta Shah** for their continuous support and for always being there to help.

I would like to thank **Dushyant Kumar** for providing all support and valuable feedback while compiling the book.

I am really very thankful to **Dinesh Verma,** CEO, **Pendown Press** and his team for their support and suggestion during the creative process.

Last but not the least, I would like to thank my wonderful wife **Deepika Chawla** for being a continuous support and encouragement during the whole process. This book and this journey would not have been possible without you –I love you…

# Chapter – 1

# How Lack of Clarity Derails Life

*Clarity is the Key for conversion to all great virtues into Reality!*

You will not be able to know the importance of clarity unless you come to know the devastating effects of ambiguity. This is indeed sheer ambiguity that gives a truly talented person run for money, translates into heavy loss for a company, ruins the prospects of a politician, turns on an ambitious Govt. project into fiasco, so on and so forth.

Just think about some unsuccessful persons you know at least for 5 years. One reason you will definitely be able to cite for their failure in life is because they kept on changing their profession/work/area of interest, etc. And you know why the spree of changes took place? Because they have no clarity. Ambiguity has engulfed that person.

Every person that comes to talk to them, every situation they face, give them an idea of doing something else, because the thing that they are doing is not producing the desired result, and they are quite excited to do something, because they think that they will be able to create a miracle the day they will change their ongoing work and start another. They become confident that "Tomorrow will be Theirs".

But, tomorrow never comes. They keep on reaping the same thing that they have been reaping, because they keep on doing with the same mindset. It is the complete lack of clarity that is creating their works mess and their life hell. Almost the entire lifetime of these kinds of person go in vain in experimenting.

Not only the individuals, companies too have to bear the brunt of ambiguity.You might also have come across with the companies offering One Stop Solution to almost all your day-to-day issues. They feel proud for being among those rare companies that have the gumption to think about almost all kinds of concerns of their clients and offer one door solution.

But, if you analyse their performance, you will come to know that their quantum of services have started diminishing with each passing year. Even though they are still claiming to provide handful number of services, it is the customer experience that will soon wipe them out of the market.

There could be a long list of examples from people/ organisation. But, the reason of the failure is just one and that is Clarity of Purpose.

## Notes:

## Chapter – 2

# Clarity Stares at your Cradle!

*To activate Clarity Level*
*from contamination;*
*one must know about*
*the Reset Button!*

***Clarity always resides in you; it's our default setting!***

The problem with Clarity is that the concept in itself seems unclear.

And the fact is, Concept of Clarity is not taught anywhere but everyone looks for it.

Let's go easy.

A basic yet profound understanding first.

The dictionary definition of Clarity is "the quality of transparency or purity".

But there are other definitions too which I have found, belong to Clarity.

Let us understand it through a scenario-

Suppose you are in a dark room that has chairs and tables in it. If you walk into such room, you will keep hitting the furniture and keep falling down. It will make you miserable. But if someone switches on the light, you can see things clearly and can walk around without hitting any furniture or falling down. Point to note here is that it's not that the furniture was not there earlier – it was there but you could not see it. The light that came brought Clarity to you to see things around.

So, Clarity is **"To See Things as It is"**, without any bias or judgement. That's it. Though this sounds simple (not as complex), but it's not easy to attain. If you are able to see things as it is and not use your own bias, beliefs, knowledge, experience, influence, etc., then you will get Clarity. It means, virtually seeing everything as just a piece of life and seeing an event only in the light of as it's happening.

Then, there is another definition of Clarity. And can be viewed through another scenario–

If there is pool of muddy water and you cannot see things clearly in it, how can you clean this muddy water to see things?

The only way is to do nothing and let the mud settle down. I am saying this with my experience. And it is also age-old wisdom.

The water gets clear because being clear is its natural state. In the same way Clarity is **"Natural State of Mind"**, just like peace and resilience falls in the category of natural state of mind.

Clarity always resides in you; it's our default setting.

Actually, our mind is naturally all clear. We bring in contaminated or opinionated thoughts (the mud) and eventually lose the clarity. If you press the default setting or reset button, you will reach the natural state and clarity will be there.

It's just like the default setting of our mobile phones.

## How!

When the mobile is procured, it comes with a basic setting so that it can perform at a level of standard productivity. But after buying the phone, we put in all extra (which is practically unnecessary) features, download irrelevant Apps, needless photos, serve-no-purpose videos, etc. All these(unnecessary) additions change the dynamics of setting. And in no time, the phone starts slowing down due to new inappropriate items being added. Now, what's the solution to get optimal functioning of the device?

## Simple

Look for the reset button or formatting. And you get the original state again.

In the same manner, you need to know where is your own reset Button and how to press it and when to press it!

# Chapter –3

# With Clarity, Great Life Unfolds

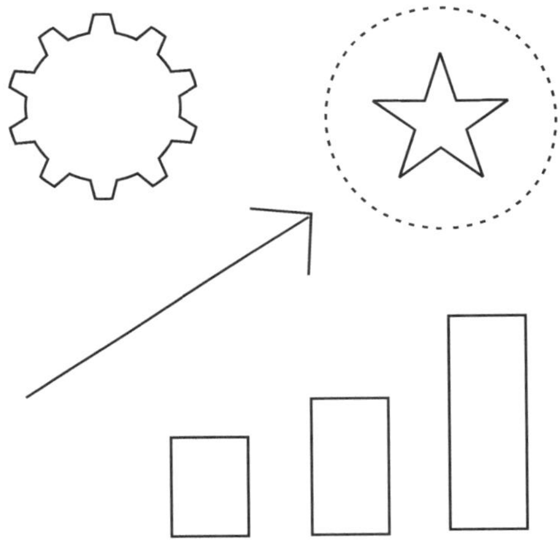

*Clarity of vision is the key to achieving your objectives*

Clarity is very important in life. If there is no clarity, the number of questions will surpass the number of answers, the number of decisions will surpass the number of options and there will be more expectations and less expected results. Be it warmth in relationship, joy in career or the ability to turn big dream into reality, all these are left to hover around us like an unfinished talk, though beginning with exuberance but trailing off when confusion comes in and interrupts the whole natural mental process.

It becomes like a person who stammers in public meeting. Though he knows how to speak well, has good knowledge about the topic he comes in to speak about, but the moment he starts speaking, he starts fumbling and the audience does not allow him to speak further and resultantly, he has to leave the stage and go behind the curtains. In fact, every person without any clarity on the things that he or she wants to do, has to go behind the curtain(has to live life that of a failure).

If your path of ambitions get clogged by umpteen number of vague plans and casual approach and half-hearted commitments, you cannot even think of reaching your goal some day. It is simply because if you do not even know as to what you are chasing, how will you be able to catch it or become even closer to accomplishing your goal?

Simply put, if you do not possess clarity, then you will not be able to get the results that you want from life seamlessly. Though, in the absence of clarity, you may still get the results by just having confidence and focus but then you arrive at that stage only by sheer chance. Not only the people will perceive, but you will also accept that your success is a fluke. You will start being apprehensive of the stability of your position. You will be like a one-film-wonder bollywood star who hardly finds mention in tabloid or people has to jog their mind to remember his/her name.

Very True, when you have clarity of your values, goals, priorities and actions, then it is always a stress-free journey of life, total in control. Only those who have clarity, can lead their lives on their terms. If you become successful to gain clarity in your life, you set better boundaries for yourself and when your boundaries become big, so becomes your achievement. More importantly, it makes your goal clear and keeps on motivating you till you reach the goal.

So, the benefits of Clarity are plenty. Some of these are given below:

- **It Makes Priorities Crystal Clear:** When confusion clears and clarity appears in your mind, your priorities become crystal clear. And when priorities become clear, you are allowed to dig deeper into what you want to do with your life.

- **Accelerated Growth:** When you get the Clarity of what exactly you want to achieve as well as about all the hurdles that may come your way, you can reach your destination in fastest time possible. These hurdles belong to time, accountability, decisions, money, relationship, people management, execution, prioritisation, leadership, etc.
- **Improved Personal and Team Productivity:** With Clarity of accountability in team, the productivity of the organisation and also of self goes up for excellence. Also, just like a machine performs the best in its default-setting, same way our mind will perform at highest level when it is in its default-state. (**read it: clarity is the natural state of mind**)
- **Your Passion Rises Like a Phoenix:** It is like opening a champagne bottle. The moment you open the Cork of Confusion what comes out violently is your passion. And when your passion becomes your job, you need not work even a single day.
- **Your Thoughts become Clear:** Clarity leads to better thoughts. Better thoughts help your create a better life, because it is your thoughts that create your reality.
- **Clarity Reduces Decision Fatigue:** Think about the decision fatigue of those who lead a life of obscurity. They experiment a lot, make decision

by the evening and revert it by the next day. On the contrary, a person with clarity makes a decision and sticks to it.

- **Clarity Paves the Way for Achieving Bigger Goals:** When you approach a goal with clarity, you get directed towards it seamlessly.
- **Peace of Mind:** With clarity, peace appears as a natural state of mind. When your mind has clarity in its natural state without contaminated thoughts, peace of mind prevails.
- **Balance in Life:** With the Clarity of when and where to utilise your time as per priorities, you achieve balance between your professional work and personal life.

**Special Bonus:** Visit www.theclarityfirst.com and click on "FREE CLARITY DECLARATION" to receive your mind-powering clarity affirmations.

- **Clear Focus:** With Clarity comes clear focus on the next actions that need to be taken or the next goal that you want to achieve.

# Chapter – 4

# Confusion, Confidence and Focus

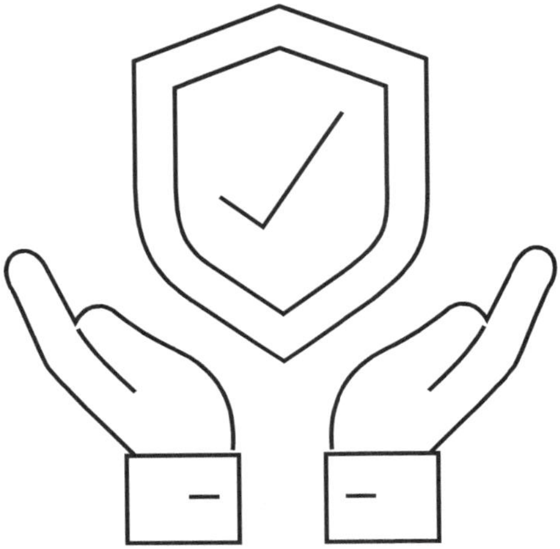

*Clarity is needed for all pursuits of life*

Get Clarity, Raise Impact!
Let's view all states, one-by-one(:)

## Confusion

Thoughts are like blowing of winds, you cannot control it unless you have attained a position where it is has become possible to control your thoughts. Even in Bhagwat Gita Arjuna said to Lord Krishna,

**"O Krishna, for me to control the mind is as impossible as to control the wind."** Of course, then Arjuna was in utter confusion, grappling for the clarity over what he should do—whether he should leave the Kurukshetra or fight for the righteous cause for the protection of Dharma.

When I meet someone and I hear that he/she is confused, I get very curious and enquire what the confusion is all about! I strongly believe that **"Confusion is not the opposite of clarity but it is the 1$^{st}$ step to Clarity"**. Because if you are confused, it only means you are looking for an answer to some problem or question. And if you start really looking for the answer, you will get it definitely by all means.

Winona Ryder, the famous American Actress has aptly said, "When you finally accept that it's OK not to have answers and it's OK not to be perfect, you realise that feeling confused is a normal part of what it is to be a human being. " So, the main challenge is not only to find the solution but discovering the real thing that you are confused about!

It's like you are walking on a road listening and enjoying music and you walk into the woods gradually. After sometime when the music stops and you look around, you come to realise that you are lost and then you look for the main road and ultimately you find it. But to make it work is not so easy.

Before finding the right direction, at first place, you must have to realise that you are actually lost (read it as state of confusion) till then. Otherwise, you don't even know you are lost and keep walking confidently.

I am sure you would have met many who have actually lost their way and are not even aware of it as they are moving in their life confidently. Confusion is very much like fault; if it is recognised, it gets corrected. If it fails to get recognised the Chaos in life continues; in fact the entire life then gets wasted because of confusion.

## Confidence

Confidence means that you can make it successfully and your feet are nerved to its accomplishments. I get intrigued when I meet confident people as they are very impressive and charismatic, with power to influence many. But with the lack of Clarity, they can create havoc in lives of many people.

As I have mentioned above, confidence only means that you are confident of your ability and you are committed to do a particular thing appreciably. But, here a point arises that "what is that particular thing?" Unless you have the clarity of that particular work, purpose, etc. it will be like strength without direction.

It will be like a drunk driver on the wheels. He is very confident of driving fast and in control but has no clarity of his act. Or consider another case of someone driving a car confidently with an unclear windshield. This is very dangerous as you see "confidence without clarity" can be harmful to self and others. This is not to say that confidence is bad, but clarity is required foremost and then confidence can be a boon. But without Clarity, confidence can be a curse. Therefore, a combination of Clarity and Confidence is what we should aspire for a smooth journey of life.

## Focus

Simply put, focus pertains to the ability to direct one's thinking in whatever direction one would intend. A state of focus means being stuck to short or long-term goals.

I often hear people saying that they are very focused in their work or business or in life. But they are not clear what they really want to achieve! It is again fruitless if it is not coupled with clarity. Suppose you are very much focused on preparing food. You do nothing in between, nothing means nothing— no phone calls, not switching on television, not even talking to your helpmate, etc. But, unless you are clear about how many people you need to feed, what kinds of food you need to prepare, etc. your whole focus on preparing best will have circular effect.

In fact, once you have the clarity of what you want to achieve, ONLY then you can actually be focused and able to achieve your goals.

***Focus without Clarity is like hitting a ball without a goalpost.***

I meet with many people who tell me candidly that whenever they know exactly what they have to do, they are able to do it effectively. They had focus but they all were only lacking clarity of what they need to achieve. Once Clarity appeared, they hit the target with precision.

## Notes:

## Chapter – 5

# That Wow Eureka Moment!

***Clarity is the revelation of your Inner Code to transform the Outer Core!***

Moments of Clarity are twinkle in the eyes with the realisation of whole Lifetime!

These are **eureka moments;** the 'light-bulb' moments when you get some idea or a solution to any problem/ question that has been bothering you for long. It usually happens when you least expect it and it lasts for few seconds only. Just after such moments, there is a feeling of ecstasy and we wonder that it was such an obvious and simple answer. But many times, we forget such moments and at times, we just act on them straightway without acknowledging and reviewing it later.

In fact, these are the **moments of clarity** that happened with Newton and Archimedes. Imagine, just a spark of clarity and great new laws were written due to that.

But never forget that the moments of clarity are not the complete solution– it's only part of the whole story. You have to stay with the result for considerable amount of time and research further. It would be a big mistake if you have got a moment of clarity and you understood that you have solved a problem.

## Birth of My Story

These moments of clarity can be very powerful and can actually change your whole life. Just see my story to find how moments of clarity transformed my life!

I had worked for 25 plus years in Software Industry at Senior Leadership Position in MNCs and Indian Companies. I had happy family, good money, powerful position, amazing success, but I was missing something. I was not sure what was missing at that time there was something telling me from inside that I am meant to achieve something else.

**Now, when I look back and assess, I realise it was Clarity that was missing in my life.**

At that time, I did not even know what I was missing!

So, as it happens with many of us, I started looking around and first thing that came to my mind was to acquire more education. So, I joined one year executive MBA program at Indian Institute of Foreign Trade, Delhi. I learned dynamics of international business as I enjoyed going to an academic institution after almost a gap of 20 years. At the end of my course, I could only say that **I got knowledge but No Clarity!**

Then, I thought I should learn new skills — maybe there are skills that I am missing and I can improve on that! So, got trainings organised on leadership, accountability, stakeholder management, assertiveness, mentoring, etc.

Similarly, at the end of such trainings, **I could say that I got the skills but still No Clarity!**

Meanwhile, I started going to many forums,

workshops, seminars organised by TIE, NASSCOM, TEDx, Josh Talks. Listening to all these wonderful speakers **I got inspired that I can do whatever I wish, but still there was No Clarity!**

I read many books of great authors, **I learnt from experiences of others but still No Clarity!**

I got mentors and a coach. They helped me to get answers to my questions and my career and skill growth. **I got lot of mentorship and support, but still No Clarity!** So, after spending almost 7 years in such knowledge-centric activities, **I got more knowledge, learnt new skills, learnt from experiences of experts, got lots of inspiration and received much needed support, but still had No Clarity of what I want to achieve!**

All this did not get me Clarity but these pursuits appeared like "dots" for me that were (just) not connected. And then a moment of clarity happened to me!

It was in January 2017 when I realised that actually I was not looking for an answer to any question – I was actually looking for a **REAL QUESTION** itself. And when that question popped up in front me I realised that this is what I need to work upon.

Do you wish to know what those eye-openers were?

Oh! Yes!! I can still recall all those steps for my new roadmap!

My Moments of Clarity

## June 2015

I was meeting my mentor, Rajesh Garodia, Pro Vice

Chancellor of Ashoka University and he asked me, "Amit, do you have any connect with Young people, I mean those who are in their20s?

I was 49 years then. And I said No (actually my only connect is with friends of my children). He told me that while going forward, now you have to deal with CEOs of diverse companies and chances are they will be much younger than you. This question made me sit up and take notice that how can I build connect with young! This simple question "do you have connect with young" made me take steps to connect with Ritesh Malik (co-founder, Innov8 co-working space) and through him I got in touch with few young entrepreneurs in the co-working space and started mentoring them and enjoying their company. This one question has now led me to coach young and dynamic minds.

## January 2017

I was attending the first coaching class to learn coaching. Our coach was Gaurav Arora (Erickson International) and he asked a group of about 20 very experienced professionals a simple question — the question was "Who are you?". For 15 odd minutes, everyone tried to answer but all in vain. And then there was pin drop silence in the room. A moment of clarity just struck me. I did not have answer to this simple question even at the age of 50. I knew then that I have to get answer to this. And I went through a process of finding it out by means of coaching, yoga, meditation and inner engineering program (of Sadhguru). I think, it took me six months and I figured out who I am (as per my own understanding) and that is:

## Peace and Balance

- Peace means "my pursuit of inner peace irrespective of what is happening outside"
- Balance means "move ahead comfortably with conflicting thoughts"

## June 2017

I was in a coaching session with a young 22-year-old entrepreneur — Shobhit Banga, the co-founder of Josh Talks. In the session the question being addressed was "What is my Life Purpose?" As we progressed and he shared the life purpose as "Unlocking Human Potential".

After the session, on my way back home, I had another moment of clarity — and that was what my life purpose is! A 22 year had so clearly stated his life purpose and such a grand one too and here I was at 51 years of age still not knowing the purpose of my life. I think it took me couple of months and I managed to get answer to the question. I defined my life purpose as:

"Walk with young, in their pursuit of Happiness and Success".

- Walk means "Coaching and Mentoring by being at equal level with the other person."
- Young means "Anyone who has deep desire to learn and evolve. Young also includes ME."
- Their pursuit of happiness and success is "Journey of the young as per their own definition of happiness and success."

Now when I coach young people, it is in line with my life purpose.

## January 2018

I was to talk to another young 25 something entrepreneur, speaker and poet, Deepak Ramola. He is on a mission to collect life lessons of all people and spread those pearls across the world through an initiative, "Project FUEL, that stands for Forward the Understanding of Every Life Lesson". A day before the call, I suddenly realised that when I will talk to him, he will say, so what is your life lesson and I had not thought of this question ever before. I just pondered for few hours on it and recalled all my life phases and penned down my one of life lesson as:

"Inner fulfilment in Life comes by Learning from All, Giving to All and No Judgement at all".

I try to follow it as far as possible Now.

## May 2018

I was having a 1-2-1 with my networking coach, Paritosh Pathak.

The question being discussed was around "what should I become?", basically around what should I be remembered as or known as. There were many things coming in like vision coach, transformation coach, purpose coach etc., but nothing was sounding right.

Then he asked a question — "What do your clients tell you after the coaching session?"

And I generally said they say that they get clarity

and actions to move forward. "Clarity, uhh!!" he said.

And somewhere deep down, I knew I was having another moment of Clarity.

After that I spend few weeks researching and stayed with the word "Clarity". Gradually, it became crystal clear to me that I will like to become and known as **Clarity Coach.**

Since then, I have made all requisite modifications in my personal branding and focused into becoming a **Business Clarity Coach.**

Now, looking back, I can say that these simple questions that came up in my moment of clarity were actually related to discovering my **own identity,** my own core; not the organisation and position that I hold; I was looking for freedom to do what I want to do; I was looking for what do I really love; I was looking for the impact that I could bring in the World.

Clarity is the revelation of your Inner Code to transform the Outer Core!

**Special Bonus:** Visit www.theclarityfirst.com and click on "Mind Empowering Poster*" based on subconscious mind- imprinting.

*Do not forget to read about Amazing Benefits subconscious mind-imprinting training.

# Chapter – 6

# I Got the Formula for Absolute Clarity!

*Consistent Craving for excellence leads to Clarity!*

Clarity is the mental calculation of success, in advance!

Based on my experience, I have devised a simple yet creative (read absolute)formula for Absolute Clarity:

$$AC_X = MC \rightarrow CC \rightarrow RC$$

Where,

**AC** – Absolute Clarity of X

**MC** – Moment of Clarity

**CC** – Consistent Commitment

**RC** – Re Check

This formula indicates that first you have to identify the task for which absolute clarity is required and here it is referred as "X".

**MC** – Moment of clarity are the moments when you have a clear mind to get a question or an answer that you are looking for in relation to "X".

**CC** – Consistent Commitment is indicating the commitment of output starting from the very moment (onset) of clarity that you need to maintain for some period of time. During this particular time, you can do more research, soul searching and see if it stays with you during it or it was only a momentarily event and vanishes eventually.

**RC** – Re-Check is that time when you revisit and recheck if that output from (the very onset) moment of clarity has actually changed or remained the same. And once it is clear then you loop back to MC.

For example, when I was looking for Absolute Clarity of my life purpose (X), I first defined it as "walk with young", and then after few months refined to "walk with young in their pursuit of happiness and success". At this point, I had thought of young as those who are less than 30 years. Later, after 3 months or so, I kept the life purpose as same but changed the definition of "young", from referring it to as less than 30 years, I changed it to "Anyone who has deep desire to learn and evolve. Young also includes me".

**Special Bonus:** Visit www.theclarityfirst.com and click on Free Video to understand this chapter on screen.

# Chapter – 7

# Solve the Puzzle via Clarity Wheel

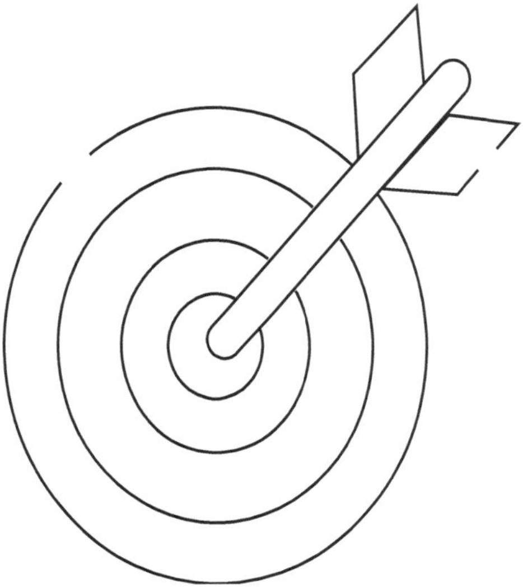

***With a clearer view, journey becomes more beautiful!***

> An investment in knowledge pays the best interest! –Benjamin Franklin

Before you start digging out more about clarity, First thing for you to do is to figure out **what you are not clear about i.e.,** find the "x" factor.

For that you can do a simple exercise:

## Step 1

**Draw a wheel with 8 spokes as shown below:**

Just write down 8 things that you are not clear about.

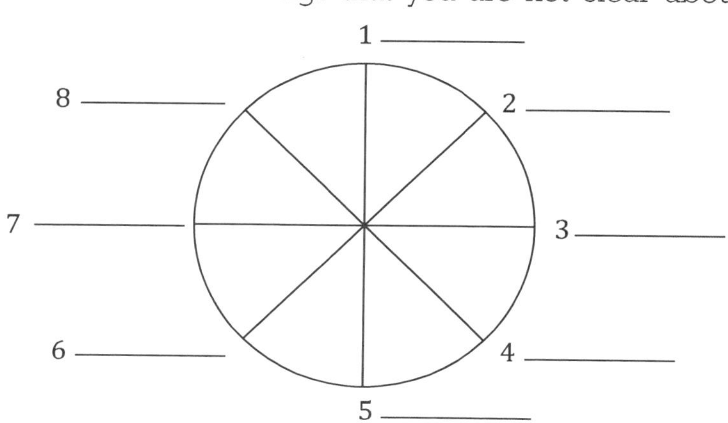

These have to be in the form of a question that starts with Why, What, How, Should, etc. Before putting the question, repeat the query to yourself 5 times – what are you not clear about in this? For example, if your question is "How do I scale my business"! Then you can ask yourself what are you really not clear about in scaling your business. And by putting that query, you may realise that you are not clear about how to get investment. Similarly, further question may be that you are not clear about your USP which would get attention of an investor to invest in your business.

Another example is that, maybe your question is "How to hire the right person for the role of Sales Head?" A slightly deeper query here could be: I know how to hire and know the skills to evaluate, but I am not clear about what are those 4-5 questions/exercises I should give him/her during interaction part by which I can judge the required skills!

## Step 2

**For the 8 questions (put up in the wheel), identify the Clarity Levels – from $L^1$ to $L^{10}$.**

Here $L^1$ is Totally Unclear (total contaminated thoughts) and $L^{10}$ is Crystal Clear (or Clarity).

## Step 3

**Identify the most important thing that you are not clear about!**

You can do that by identifying the question of which clarity level if increased by 1 level, it would improve clarity levels of most of the other 7 questions also.

Now you have identified the most important question that was not clear to you (answer was also not clear). And when you were able to find the answer to that question, you would be getting a feeling of peace and contentment.

## Step 4

Now, with this question, identify the desired clarity level that you want and also identify 3 to 5 things that are stopping you to move from Current Clarity Level to the **Desired Clarity Level.**

See picture below:

<Most Important Question that you are not clear about>

Now with this exercise, you got insight to identify the most important thing that is not clear to you, its current clarity level, the desired clarity level and what is stopping you (factor/s) to move to the desired clarity level.

In itself, this is very first step and start of your journey of Absolute Clarity.

**Notes:**

## Chapter – 8

# 4 WAY to Highway!

*An expert is an agent of change that works not for your strategy but on you as strategy!*

Compass of Clarity not only gives directions; essentially navigates the entire route!

Glad that you have found what is the most important thing that is not clear to you and what stops you IN YOUR SUCCESS!

Now, it's time for the approach to handle it.

Believe me, this part is very simple; not complex.

There are Four Approaches you can use:

## Approach 1:

### Do Nothing!

This does not mean no action-no response. Rather, it means "awareness". There is much possibility that while going through the process itself, you will get awareness and your questions get sorted out. It's like mirage — the very first time you see mirage while driving a car, you get hallucinated. But after becoming aware that it's only a mirage- illusion and not real water; then every next time while driving your car you come across a mirage, you do nothing — just keep driving normally.

## Approach 2

### Do Something-Find an Expert

Search to find an expert, mentor or a coach. For questions that mainly relates to skill development, seek someone who is an expert in that field! You can also look for a mentor or a coach to support you and get answer to the question.

## Approach 3

### Do Something – ME Time

This is my personal favourite. To find answer to the most important question that is not clear to you, do a ME time for 30 minutes.

The process is very simple.

Just sit somewhere where there are no distractions (no phone, noise, etc.) with a pen, blank notepad and timer.

Put the question on the top of the page, start the timer and just write all thoughts coming up in relation to that question.

It's important to get the thoughts out from the virtual world of mind to the physical world (to write on paper).

During this process, if you come across any actions, then also note them down on a separate sheet.

Make sure you spend complete 30 minutes.

Many times, I have seen people finishing this task earlier.

It indicates probably they have got the wrong question.

Because, in my view, for the most important question of one's life (and which is not clear) one has to mandatorily spend at least 30 minutes thinking about it (if one really needs scientific result).

At the end of this exercise, you must have most of your thoughts and actions noted down on paper. You can do the same exercise each day continuously for a week and I am sure you would have got enough actions to get clarity with your own effort.

Now, it's time to execute the action.

## Approach 4

### Take the advantage of THE CLARITY EXPERT

Never delay your Progress due to Process!

What If none of the approach works for you!

Then, I appreciate your effort to connect with me as **Your Business Clarity Coach.**

Because you can't leave your ongoing goal to excel in the mid of journey!

I am a dedicated whole-time professional Clarity Coach who whole-heartedly takes care of every aspiration, dream and possibility that lies in every individual.

But my humble suggestion is that before reaching out to me, give a try to other approaches first. In fact, this will warm up your effort for a greater transformation on the way.

## Notes:

# Chapter – 9

# Coaching is Car; Consulting and Training are Tyres!

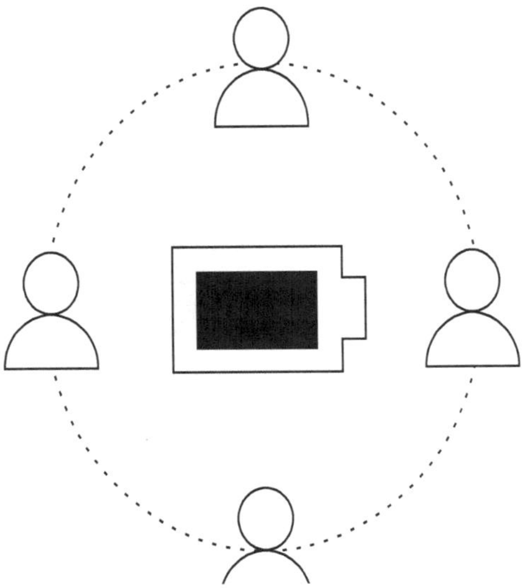

*" Leadership is more about responsibility than ability!"*

Coaching is a hidden necessity to create Phenomenal Success!

I am referred many times as a Business Consultant and I get invites to do training programs. But I am not a consultant or a trainer, in that very sense. I am, in fact, truly more than that! But before reaching to my core, let's quickly find the difference between consulting, training and coaching.

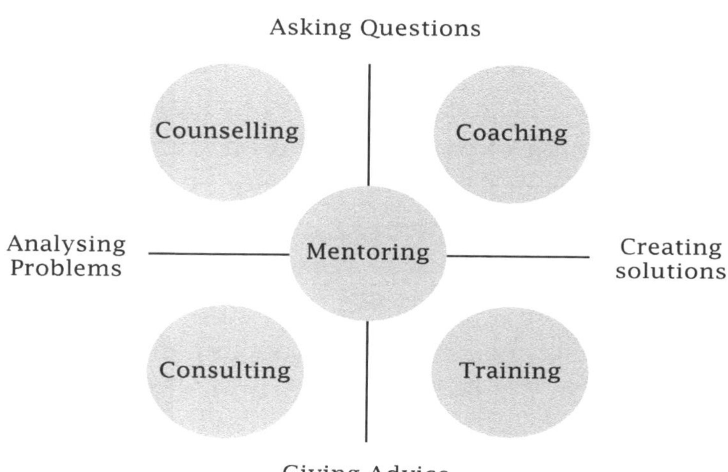

The picture above shows the difference between coaching and other types of learning modes. While Coaching is about creating solutions by asking questions, we have Training as a creating solution by giving advice. Same way Consulting is analysing problem and giving advice.

While in all the cases, intent is same or similar but the approach is quite different.

It is very interesting to know the difference between Coaching and Consulting because many potential business players just miss the ball due to misunderstanding in choosing the wrong pitch.

It's Versus Game: Coaching Vs. Consulting

**Coaching can help turn an entrepreneur into a great leader.**

Consulting, on the other hand, provides that much-needed expertise and assistance.

In coaching, answers and solutions are self-generated by the client with the coach as facilitator; in consulting, answers and solutions are provided by the consultant as a subject matter expert. While the end result is similar supporting client's learning, choices and right action yet the approach and process are quite different.

## Instruction Vs. Guidance

The main difference between coaching and consulting is that coaching pulls out answers from the client while consulting instructs the client what to do. With coaching, you walk away with strategies to uncover your truth (close to your heart) on your own. With consulting, you get ready tools that can assist you in moving forward and executing.

A consultant would ride the bicycle for a while and write a "how to" manual for you. A coach would get you ride on the bicycle and walk alongside you, guiding you through the process until you feel confident enough to ride on your own.

Hire a consultant when you want to learn a process or method.

**But, Hire a coach when you want to discover yourself and follow it for true success.**

Outside Expertise or Internally-Driven Growth

A Consultant is usually a subject matter expert who offers technical and professional advice to clients based on his understanding, knowledge and experience. A Coach, however, helps clients find their own clarity to dig answers and assists them to understand how to move forward in achieving their goals and grow personally.

## Exploring Vs. Providing Possibilities

When you coach, you explore possibilities.

When you consult, you provide possibilities.

Knowing this difference enables you to provide the greatest value to your customer. When you're coaching, you help them explore possibilities for themselves that they might not be able to see. When you consult, you take those possibilities and provide them with options based on your knowledge and experience.

## Recommendation Vs. Exploration

Consultants diagnose a problem and make a recommendation. From there, they take the client to a place on the basis of what they believe is best!

Coaches do not diagnose problems; rather they partner with clients to determine the biggest questions they want to explore plus create an experience for the client to arrive at their own answers, based on what the client himself believes will work best!

## Asking Questions Vs. Providing Solutions

There is a clear distinction between Coach and Consultant.

A good Coach is a good listener; they let silence do the work. They focus to understand through thoughtful and sincere inquiry without judgement. And they guide the client to see solutions for themselves by asking, and not forceful telling.

Consultants, on the other hand, provide ready solutions while consulting.

**But it's been proved that Long-lasting clarity and growth come from within, not from outside source.**

Different Approach with The Same Intent

In Coaching, answers or solutions appear from the client with the power of coach as facilitator.

Though in Consulting, answers or solutions are projected by the consultant as area under discussion expert.

Interestingly, the end result is similar — supporting client's learning, choices and right action yet the approach and process are quite dissimilar.

## Focus on Problem or On Client?

The key difference between Coaches and Consultants is where the focus is! In consulting, the focus is on the problem and the consultant offers best practices to address the problem. In coaching, the focus is on the client and on helping them to reach to their core. Coach tap into the client's own ability to solve the challenges and problems that emerge in work and life.

## Difference Lies in Who the Expert Is

Coaches assume the client is the expert in their business and life. Through active inquiry and thought-provoking questions, a coach helps the client in solving their specific issues.

However, with a consultant, (problem is) they are the assumed expert. Understand this. It is important because coaching produces meaningful and lasting changes over the short and long-term time zone, whereas consulting is generally able to offer short-term answers to a specific problem.

One more understanding: **Coaching Vs. Training**

Essentially, Training is about transferring knowledge while Coaching is about enhancing knowledge (or development, in simple words). Training is done by attending training courses or by reading a book or by watching videos and so many other modules of learning.

It's about knowledge being transferred by one entity to another.

On the other hand, Coaching is a process for enhancing your knowledge. Coaching is done by asking meaningful questions while training is more of giving already existing answers.

Training is also more structured with fixed agenda and content; while in Coaching, it's a flexible conversational mode with agenda and content defined by the client only and emerged in natural way (so of more intrinsic value).

Basically, in Coaching there is more accountability (or authenticity) quotient generated during transformation of the client as the solutions and action comes from the client only. From my experience, I can tell that it's such an amazing feeling when the clients discover their own solution while conversing with the coach. Their solutions are always better than what I would have suggested and have much better probability of execution as self-accountability is involved here with real magnitude.

Many times, I have clients who have gone through consulting or have consultants working for them and they are going through some training too. They wonder if they need a coach at that point of time.

Well! Coaching can easily co-exist with Training and Consulting.

Don't you agree on that?

Let me share how that works!

You go for some training course or you read a book

or watch an educational video. Most of the time people take these knowledge shots and then come back and do nothing about it.

I encourage my clients to pick 2-3 actions that they would like to implement in their lives. Such identified actions then can be brought into the Coaching process.

On practical front, let's see how it works!

Once, I had a client and we were working on the accountability structure of the organisation. The client had also recently gone for a training program where a standardised organisation structure was taught. He wanted to implement all of it. We included that idea in the Coaching session, and after some challenging questions and conversation, we refined the structure and implemented immediate applicable part of the learning. And it worked successfully. The part missing in the training is complemented by the Coaching.

I am being reminded of the great words of **Albert Einstein:**

**I never teach my pupil, I only provide the conditions in which they can learn.**

I like to adopt this league of performance.

**Notes:**

# Chapter-10

# Decoding Clarity Coaching

*Coaching is the ladder;*
*Clarity Coaching is*
*the Escalator!*

***Knowledge is asking the Right Question;
Genius is offering the Real Question!***

It is clear from all the above, the base of Clarity Coaching is about only two things:

## Discovering the REAL Question

It's not about finding solution or answer but actually finding the real question that needs to be addressed. Solution is easy but finding the real (not right, **but Real**) question is the intent of clarity coaching.

I love to play around with the question — as the question evolves, more and more possibilities open up. Once the real question emerges, then finding solution for it becomes the matter of expertise. In the last three decades of my evaluation of hundreds of business and personal profiles, I came to the conclusion:

Solution most of the time lies at the tail of the problem

There are few tips to dig the base about REAL QUESTION:

- Should have positive tone and words
- Should be looking at future and focused on solution
- Should be open-ended so that can open up (even) distinct possibilities
- Should be in your control and within your accountability

**Let me throw more light on this:**

Some examples of good real questions, that I have encountered in my coaching journey are like:

- How do I keep myself motivated daily?
- What am I doing today?
- How do I challenge my business partner and still maintain relationship?
- How can we have shared vision and culture?
- Which is the best business idea for me to pursue?
- How do I define growth?
- What do I need to change to retain top talent in my company?
- What I need to improve in myself to be extremely successful?
- What should I do to become disciplined?
- How do I find time for myself on daily basis?
- How do I say No and not feel guilty?
- How do I get ready to change my profession after a prolonged innings?

- How can I utilise my time more effectively?
- How can I create future leaders?
- What should I do to let go of control?
- What is my life purpose?
- What should be the vision of my company?

## Identifying SMART Actions

It's important that after a personalised clarity coaching session or a group coaching session, 3-5 actions need to be identified. Then, Actions should follow the age-old simple principle of SMART.

**Specific**

**Measurable**

**Achievable**

**Relevant**

**Time Bound**

## S – Specific

The actions should be clear and specific, otherwise you won't be able to focus on your efforts or feel truly motivated to achieve it. To meet this need, you can try to answer the five "W" questions:

- What do I want to accomplish?
- Why is this action important?
- Who is involved?
- Where is it located?
- Which resources or limits are involved?

## M – Measurable

It's important to have measurable actions, so that you can track your progress and stay motivated. Assessing progress on regular basis helps you to stay focused, meeting your deadlines, and feeling the excitement of getting closer to achieving them. A measurable action should address questions such as:

### How much?

How many?

How will I know when it is accomplished?

## A – Achievable

Your action also needs to be realistic and attainable to be successful. In other words, it should stretch your abilities but still prevail under your command. When you set an achievable goal, only then (sometimes) you may be able to identify previously overlooked opportunities or resources that can bring you closer to it.

An achievable action will usually answer questions such as:

- How can I accomplish this action?

- How realistic is the action, based on other constraints, such as financial factors?

## R – Relevant

This step is about ensuring that your action matters to you and that it also aligns with other appropriate goals that you may have.

A relevant action can answer "yes" to these questions:

- Does this seem worthwhile?
- Is this the right time?
- Does this match our other efforts/needs?
- Am I the right person to reach this goal?
- Is it applicable in the current socio-economic environment?

## T – Time Bound

Every action needs a target time slot, so that you have a deadline to focus on and something to work towards it. This helps to prevent everyday task domination over your long-term goals.

A time bound action will usually answer these questions:

- When?
- What can I do six months from now?
- What can I do six weeks from now?
- What can I do today?

There is another very important element attached to the Action and that is the **"commitment level"** to perform the action. The noted action is actually like a commitment made to oneself and one has to own that commitment. I have come across many clients who write down a clear action but later do not execute and are able to provide many reasons for it. So, for each action commitment, level of $L^9$ to $L^{10}$ is required.

## Notes:

## Chapter – 11

# Attaining Clarity–Do It Yourself (DIY) Way

*Coaching is the powerhouse of creativity to unleash continuous Success!*

According to Richie Norton, the author of the Amazon bestselling book The Power of Starting Something Stupid, "Intentional living is the art of making our own choices before others' choice make us". But, unless there is clarity, intentional living will be a far cry.

Given below is the 8 Do It Yourself Ways to attain clarity:

- **Write down on Papers:** Our memory is like a leaky bucket. You cannot expect "come and remain for lifetime" from your memory. Almost all successful self-improvement writers(Zig Ziglar, Brian Tracy, Anthony Robbins, etc.) have talked about the importance of having written goals. When you write about your goal, you make it transformed from Vague to Valid.

  A written goal is also very powerful in the sense that you can keep it close to your chest and whenever you feel yourself off the track, you can open it. It will help you come back on the right track.

- **Work on your Passions:** Identify yourself. Who you are. Write down your passion statements for your work and life. If you identify your passion, you will get saved from making hasty decisions about your life. Do what you do the best, leave others to have the rest. Make your passion your profession and you will not have to work even a single day.
- **Avoid Multitasking:** I heard people saying, "I love multitasking, multitasking is in my gene, I hate doing only one thing at a time" so on and so forth. But, I have got good reasons to believe that multitasking not only prevents you from being perfect in the work that you do, but it does also distract you and takes a heavy toll on your clarity goal.
- **Eliminate Distractions:** If you are willing to attain clarity in your life and you are in the seas of distractions, that means you are expecting fruits from a tree that does not have even a single leaf. Therefore, visualise your morning routine—do you get surrounded by newspaper, mobile, television, kids, etc.? If yes, ensure that you get at least 15 minutes' time for yourself every day. Moreover, if you come to know that most of your distractions are self-created, it will become easier for you to get them eliminated.
- **Be in Peace with Yourself:** Get a minimum of 5 minutes for yourself out of your busy schedule. Utilise that time to its optimum use. Make it

thought-less, emotion less, do not allow any thought to peep in for that period. Just be with yourself. Cleanse your Mind, meditate, dispel all kinds of distractions, mental clutter.

- **Write your Clarity Statements:** No matter whether you have achieved some clarity or not, keep declaring that you have attained clarity on something, like how to make your morning tea-free, how to start the day, what kinds of thought to entertain, what to expel, so on and so forth. If you keep on writing these kinds of statements, your subconscious mind will help you achieve this one day.
- **Challenge your Impossible:** Make a list of what you think "it is impossible for you". You can have in list "I cannot get up at 5 AM, I can leave my life, but not cigarette, I can never be a vegetarian, I can never be a businessperson, etc." Now, look at the list and visualise as if your enemy is making mockery of you for not being able to do the things listed there. Once you are able to visualise such things, your cells will become active to making these "impossible" into "possible." And the day will come when the list will be sans any entry of impossible.
- **Take Help of a Clarity Coach:** If nothing of the above works and you start feeling yourself very low in self confidence and wretched, take help of a clarity coach. A clarity coach knows hundred times more than what is mentioned here. He will

be the perfect doctor of your kind of ailment, because by just spending few minutes with you, he will be able to quantify your problem and then and there your treatment process will start. Subsequently, you will emerge as a person with clarity.

# Call of the Future!

*Future belongs to those who are clear about their Present!*

The Business Clarity Coaching Programs will help you and your company achieve the escape velocity to move into a new orbit, with absolute clarity, confidence, focus and courage.

So far, so good!

To have Clarity in Life and in other realms of Creative Areas of Work Life, It's essential for future.

As the insights into the World of Clarity have opened up new dimensions for brilliant performance and leading an empowered life, I extend my hand for a meaningful interaction, NOW.

I personally invite every entrepreneur, would-be entrepreneur and happy to be entrepreneur as well everyone who wishes to feel the power of Clarity Coaching to transform the very approach to attain heights of excellence.

Feel free to drop into my office for a cup of coffee or fix up a conference call or any other innovative way (if you have) to meet, interact and Go Higher to scale the Desired.

My available options are given below:

## Clarity Hive

A-304, Pioneer Urban Square
Golf Course Extension Road, Sector 62
Gurgaon - 122002, Haryana (India)

amit@amitchawla.coach

+ 91 956 005 5280

in https://www.linkedin.com/in/amit-chawla-coach/